IT'S TIME TO EAT NOPAL

It's Time to Eat NOPAL

Walter the Educator

Silent King Books
A WhichHead Entertainment Imprint

Copyright © 2025 by Walter the Educator

All rights reserved. No part of this book may be reproduced in any manner whatsoever without written per- mission except in the case of brief quotations embodied in critical articles and reviews.

First Printing, 2024

Disclaimer

This book is a literary work; the story is not about specific persons, locations, situations, and/or circumstances unless mentioned in a historical context. Any resemblance to real persons, locations, situations, and/or circumstances is coincidental. This book is for entertainment and informational purposes only. The author and publisher offer this information without warranties expressed or implied. No matter the grounds, neither the author nor the publisher will be accountable for any losses, injuries, or other damages caused by the reader's use of this book. The use of this book acknowledges an understanding and acceptance of this disclaimer.

It's Time to Eat NOPAL is a collectible early learning book by Walter the Educator suitable for all ages belonging to Walter the Educator's Time to Eat Book Series. Collect more books at WaltertheEducator.com

USE THE EXTRA SPACE TO TAKE NOTES AND DOCUMENT YOUR MEMORIES

NOPAL

It's time to eat, oh, what a treat!

It's Time to Eat

Nopal

A special food so fresh and neat!

Green and crisp, so fun to see,

Nopal is so good for me!

It comes from cactus, big and tall,

With little spines, don't touch at all!

But when it's cleaned and chopped up right,

It makes a dish that's pure delight!

Slice it thin or chop it small,

Cook it soft or not at all!

Boil, grill, or fry it, too,

So many ways, what will you do?

Mix with eggs or in a stew,

Put it in a taco, too!

With cheese and beans or on my plate,

Every bite just tastes so great!

It's Time to Eat

Nopal

A little slimy? That's okay!

A squeeze of lime will wash away.

With onions, peppers, colors bright,

A dish so fresh and full of might!

One big bite, crunch, crunch, crunch!

I can eat this for my lunch!

Chewy, tasty, soft, and fun,

Eating nopal, yum, I'm done!

Try a salad, cool and light,

With juicy tomatoes, what a sight!

Or in a soup, so warm and nice,

A special taste that adds some spice!

Grandma says, "It's good for you!"

Helps me run and jump so true!

Strong and healthy, big and bright,

It's Time to Eat

Nopal

Nopal makes me feel just right!

One more bite, I love it so,

It helps my body grow and grow!

A food so tasty, fresh, and fun,

Nopal time for everyone!

So let's all eat and share a smile,

This cactus food is full of style!

Green and yummy, soft or tall,

It's Time to Eat

Nopal

Hooray for nopal, I love it all!

ABOUT THE CREATOR

Walter the Educator is one of the pseudonyms for Walter Anderson. Formally educated in Chemistry, Business, and Education, he is an educator, an author, a diverse entrepreneur, and he is the son of a disabled war veteran. "Walter the Educator" shares his time between educating and creating. He holds interests and owns several creative projects that entertain, enlighten, enhance, and educate, hoping to inspire and motivate you. Follow, find new works, and stay up to date with Walter the Educator™

at WaltertheEducator.com

www.ingramcontent.com/pod-product-compliance
Lightning Source LLC
LaVergne TN
LVHW052013060526
838201LV00059B/4014